The Other-Side

Of

Worship

Sonja A. Bell

Published by D. Auguste & Associates, LLC.

www.daapco.com

Printed in the United States of America

TABLE OF CONTENTS

Page

Chapter   **Page**

Chapter   **Page**

ACKNOWLEDGEMENTS

Thank you to my sisters Missy and Shonda and to all of my family for your support. To my sons Ivory; CJ, and Jeremy, and my daughter-in-law Nacotia, I know It was not easy in the natural, but I continued to see faith in your eyes as you made sure to connect with me every day. Thank you for keeping the laughter around; for singing and worshipping the Lord with me. Normally I would plan and make preparation for the family Sunday dinners and fun games, but watching as you carried on blessed me so much. I love and appreciate each of you.

To Pastors Al & Didrea Moore and the entire Westgate Church Family, thank you for walking this journey with my family and I in faith and for carrying us in the spirit. I am forever grateful for your unwavering love, prayers and support.

A Special Acknowledgement

A special thanks to *B. Lynn Davis*. When I came to you, I had no idea of how to begin writing a book.

You mentored me and walked me through the steps of learning how to write my story. Along the journey you continued to be an inspiration and this allowed me to see more of the ability God has given me to write and inspire others.

DEDICATION

This book is dedicated to my mother, Mary Bell. A very special acknowledgment to you Mama for being the woman of God you are and have been in my life. You are a warrior in the spirit and a strong intercessor. You are also a worshipper. Only because of your relationship with God could you continue to stand in faith no matter what you saw going on with me or what you heard the doctors say about me.

I thank you for being a good caregiver and making all the sacrifices you did to take care of me. I'm so grateful for you being so much more than a good caregiver. You spoke the word of God (life) into me continuously, worshipping God and praying for and with me. My prayer is for other caregivers taking care of love ones to be encouraged as they read this book. To keep trusting God even through situations that seem hopeless as you did.

I'm reflecting on hearing you say these words; may they inspire others as well…

To worship your way out, it's not something that's passive; you have to have a relationship with Him, know His voice, no matter where you are or what you are going through, you can worship because you know God has already provided."

-Mary Bell

INTRODUCTION

"O Lord my God, I cried out to You, And You healed me."

Psalms 30:2 (NKJV)

What do you think about this scripture from the Bible concerning healing? Do you believe it is real to apply in your life for today, or do you believe this scripture is a part of history and only applied to writers inspired by God or the characters in bible stories?

My purpose for writing this book is to share my story and testimony about the love of God and how He is the healer of a broken heart; a broken spirit, and the healer of all sickness and disease. God is also a restorer; a redeemer, and the God of miracles, signs, and wonders.

To the patient and the caregiver of loved ones going through a battle with an illness; there is healing and fullness of joy in His presence.

I pray that this book points the reader to Him, who is the author and finisher of my faith.

Chapter One

Here is My Story

I remember during the latter part of 2011 experiencing fatigue and continuing to push myself. You know how we can do sometimes, especially as mothers, we keep going because we think we must get more done. God forbid that we stop to take a break, even when all the red flags are up. We can get signals constantly from our body, and yet, we keep moving to take care of others without the thought of taking better care of ourselves.

As the New Year, January 2012 came, I was still moving at that fast pace pushing through fatigue. As you know, when you don't rest properly your immune system will get weak and eventually things will start to catch up with you. I thought I had a cold and later I started experiencing vertigo.

From my primary doctor, I was sent from specialist to specialist trying to find out what was going on and causing the different symptoms I was having.

The thought occurred to me to take a leave from work but, instead I kept going not taking time to look further into what was going on. Using my sick days at work when needed was my solution, but I was not a priority on my list.

Three months into the year had come so quickly and yet I was continuously too busy to stop and check on myself. I'm sure there are some of you reading my story and you see yourself.

You may be currently ignoring your body in pursuit of being an overachiever. This can take its toll on you after a while, there's only so much our body can take when it comes to neglecting it. This is like driving your car, when you see warning signals, this indicates a problem.

However, continuing to drive and ignoring warnings in a car will not make the problem go away. Furthermore, damage can occur in the engine of the car, malfunctions can happen electronically.

Sometimes we may even come to a place where the car will not start. Well, this can happen to us, physically we can shut down if we don't stop to look further into warning signals our body may give us.

"Come to Me, all you who labor and are heavy laden, and I will give you rest."

Matthew 11:28 (KJV)

Chapter Two

The Engine Attempted to Stall

As I mentioned, when we neglect to take care of our body, it's similar to not taking care of a car. There are several reasons why a car will stall. It can be issues with the air flow, fuel, or mechanics. Some common reasons we know could be running out of gas, the engine overheating, the battery dies, the starter may need to be replaced, etc.

This analogy of the car engine best describes in some way what happened to me in March 2012. It was a Friday evening just leaving work and I was exhausted. I felt like my tank was on empty. I was running on fumes and it was nobody's fault but my own. Sometimes we overload ourselves because we don't say no when we should.

Other times we add to our plate a special project or multiple good ideas that may not be from the Lord.

"But those who wait on the Lord Shall renew their strength; They shall mount up with wings like eagles, They shall run and not be weary, They shall walk and not faint."

Isaiah 40:31 (KJV)

So, there I was at the end of the week and I had a women's retreat to attend for the weekend. The thought came to my mind to rest Friday and join the retreat Saturday or go to the room and sleep a while and join later that night. I never told anyone how I was feeling physically. To be honest, I hadn't been feeling well for two weeks prior. There were some medical issues, but I kept adding and allowing things on my plate instead of resting.

Truly at that point, I thought it's too late to stop now to rest and I was too excited about the retreat.

Arriving at the location of the retreat brought great anticipation for the weekend. Once settled in with the luggage in the rooms, we had a meeting, dinner, and the evening sessions. It was such a Blessing!

Later that night I talked most of the night with a roommate. It was great conversation about the Lord and family history, but it was not wisdom. I needed to rest. I finally went to sleep for barely two hours.

During my prayer time early that Saturday morning, the Lord began to instruct me to pray the prayer of protection over all of us attending the retreat.

He specifically had me to come against a spirit of death in intercession. I obeyed and prayed as instructed although my mind wondered if everyone was alright; nevertheless, I trusted the Lord to do as He was leading me to do.

I prayed over the conference as so many others were and had been for weeks prior as well. I truly believe with all my heart by God's grace and mercy, he instructed me to pray against what the enemy wanted to happen. God can see ahead of us and he spoiled the enemy's plan.

The morning sessions of the retreat were great. It was time for the altar call after a teaching session on deliverance. When I finished singing, "No Weapon" by Fred Hammond during the time of ministry, my mother came up to hug me and prayed over me. She said the Spirit of the Lord instructed her to do so and she obeyed.

As she walked away from me, I noticed from her waist down was pure white like a sheet was draped from her waist to the floor. Gradually, the white moved up higher and higher until I could no longer see my mother nor anyone else in the room.

At this moment, I realized something was wrong, but I could not speak.

Hoping someone would notice, I heard one of the praise team members ask another, "Is she ok?" I could not feel my body, but I could hear perfectly.

A crashing sound rang out in my ear and I realized it was me falling. I fell on someone standing behind me taking them down underneath me. From the sounds I heard, I knew someone was injured. "Oh my God, did I hurt someone?" This was my immediate thought soon followed by wondering what was happening to me.

I heard footsteps rushing toward me and familiar voices, including my mother, asking me to open my eyes, to squeeze her hand, and to move my legs. I could not verbally respond although I thought I was doing as they asked of me.

Chapter Three

The Most Beautiful Sound in My Ear

As I continued to hear those I know call my name and talk to me, someone whispered in my ear the words, "*Worship Your Way Out*". I remember reaching out to God from my heart and trying to push past the fear of not knowing what was going on.

The familiar voices around me became dim and slowly faded into a soft background. In my hearing was the most beautiful worship I ever heard.

Voices worshipping the Lord; men and women, mature and younger voices all together, I could hear singing. The voices sounded like instruments were in them.

The sounds seemed to float on air like it was dancing. At certain moments, someone's voice would peek out to lead and fade back in with everyone. This happened without directives, there were no overlaps or clashing into who would peek out next to sing. They all seemed to just know when it was their turn and yet with such oneness.

As I began to join in singing with them, my thoughts were, "I know this beautiful song too, wow!", "*When did they learn this?*", "*We need to sing this at church*". I didn't remember at that time, this is a women's retreat. There are no men in the congregation to sing.

Days later, when the worship team came to visit me in the hospital, I asked them about the song. The singers looked at me strangely and said, "*There wasn't a song, we were concerned about you and praying that you would be alright*".

I realized, no one was singing in the chapel that day. When I was singing, they heard unclear sounds of gibberish. However, in my hearing, I was worshipping with the congregation of people.

The Lord allowed me to hear a little of the most beautiful heavenly worship. It was such a sweet sound in my ear, but it was also filled with so much unity, love, peace, and joy. I saw nothing with my eyes, but from my hearing, God allowed me to hear and somehow see with my ears, the beauty of worshipping Him.

Chapter Four

While Lifted Up

There I was being removed from the ambulance to a helicopter on my way to the hospital. I had no idea what was going on with me, but I knew it was serious for all this to be happening. In my heart, I began to pray. Asking God to cover the travel in the helicopter, to protect me, and let me be alright.

I thought of my immediate family and church family, wondering how they were. I don't remember the duration of the ride to the emergency room. I do remember praying in the Spirit on the inside of me, and covering in prayer all that was going on.

It was unbelievable that I was in a helicopter. What was happening? I prayed asking God to remove fear.

On arrival to the trauma unit, the staff started immediately rushing me in and cutting my clothes. I remember thinking, I just purchased this cute skirt.

Thinking of the skirt at that time may have seemed like the last thing for me to be thinking about. However, focusing on the skirt helped me to remove my thoughts from the seriousness of the situation I was in.

At some point I realized I could not move my left side; it hadn't occurred to me until later. My left side had no feeling or sense of touch. Even the left side of my face had a drooping look which I was told, was because of the muscles in the left side of my face collapsing.

So many things were going on at one time, I saw nurses and doctors rushing, and moving fast and they seem to fade away as though I fell asleep.

It wasn't sleep or maybe it was, all I know is I was in a place of peacefulness.

The worship was so beautiful, the music like nothing I've experienced; such a peaceful floating feeling.

My mother was allowed to come in to see me. Later she told me, my right hand was lifted waving from side to side worshipping.

Chapter Five

Unclear Diagnosis and Something Unexpected

There were so many tests done on me. The doctors could not come to a decision as to what caused this nor could they give a diagnosis. The symptoms were a mixture of different things they said associated with stroke and seizure, but they couldn't understand why the oxygen was not flowing to my brain.

As they continued to run test and administer meds intravenously to do more test, there was an error made. Someone overlooked what was already given to me and gave the medicine to me again.

Moments later my blood pressure began to drop; the beeping signals on the hospital monitors went off. The nurse dropped the clipboard and ran out of the room to go get help.

My mother was calling my name and slapping my hand trying to get me to respond. Then I heard her voice leave from the side of the bed, although I could not respond to her. I heard her praying in the Spirit a short distance away.

Then I heard the hospital staff come back in the room and someone said "*we must get her pressure to come back up*". I heard them tell my mother they needed to tilt the bed upside down as much as possible.

I heard my mother ask, is her pressure going back up and they said yes with a sigh of relief they responded to my mother. All the beeping stopped, and the room was calm again.

Later, my mother shared with me she had to step away from the bed to remove herself from what she saw in the natural to pray and intercede for me.

She knew whatever was going on at that moment, God was going to give a breakthrough in that situation and He did.

Chapter Six

"All This Medicine Must Stop"

At some point, the feeling in my left arm returned, but it was still very weak. The muscle structure on the left side of my face returned but it was still very numb. I had no sense of touch. I also eventually began to feel pain in my left leg. When the feeling returned in my leg, the doctor ordered test to be done on it. The test discovered a fracture in my leg.

While still waiting to be diagnosed throughout all this time, the doctors prescribed medications to treat the different symptoms. It felt like I was the object of an experiment. Although they meant well, they didn't know for sure what to do for me.

The doctors explained to my family that the best they could do is treat the symptoms. This method caused me to be on multiple prescriptions. I was taking seven meds during the day and six meds at night. The medications made me drowsy and lethargic. I was hardly able to function in conversation.

One day, my mother, who was my primary caregiver as well as the person always close by my side praying over me and speaking the Word of God over me said, "*All this medicine must stop!*"

She started praying over the medicine and rebuking side effects of the medicine and she confessed the Word of God over the medicine. She did this faithfully morning and night before I took the medicine.

There was a determination and a diligence in my mother. No matter what it looked like, she knew things would get better. All the medicine that I was taking would not be always.

Although medical staff shared with her I would be on the meds the rest of my life, she knew better because she believed in the report of the Lord concerning me. I remember hearing her say, "If it doesn't line up with the Word of God, it's not so!"

Chapter Seven

A Different Form of Rehab

Two weeks later, I was discharged from the hospital and sent to a local rehab facility. This is where I was given a daily routine of occupational and physical therapy. However, I was not able to do the daily routine due to the medical issues.

I continued to have mini strokes due to not getting enough oxygen to the brain. I was there for a period of four weeks getting in the therapy as I could. There were good days when I could get in some of the occupational and physical therapy, but this happened toward the end of the duration being there. Unfortunately, most of the time, I was unable to do the therapy prescribed.

I remember one time they stood me to my feet all I had to do was take five steps, but this was too difficult.

Trying to walk was like running a marathon I could hardly catch my breath. After getting lightheaded, they had to tilt the wheelchair upside down for a period of time. They said this was to allow blood (oxygen) to flow to my brain. This all happened while pressing to take five steps; however, there were different forms of therapy that motivated my desire to push to get better.

The prayer and worship done with me each day was therapy. My sons visiting, family and friends also coming to see me was more encouraging than they realized.

A very special form of therapy was my first grand-daughter, Karah Sonje'... She was born two months prior to this happening to me. Jeremy and Cotia, her parents would bring her as often as they could, along with my other grand-children.

Although I was too weak to hold her, Karah was placed on me each visit. I can't explain it but the moment she was placed on me, my love for her was released with the most peaceful feeling. You see, she was an answer to prayer, after twenty-two years of all boys born between my siblings and I and grandchildren, my son's prayer was answered. She was a reminder of God's faithfulness. My desire to get better to hold her and comb her hair and make things for her grew.

Finally, the end of four weeks came; I was discharged from the rehab center to return home. After returning home, there were a few complications in making the adjustments. Medically, things were not staying consistent with me.

Eventually, I had to be readmitted back into the hospital.

I was there in the hospital again wondering would this get better for me. After two weeks, I was stronger and showed improvements and was discharged home again.

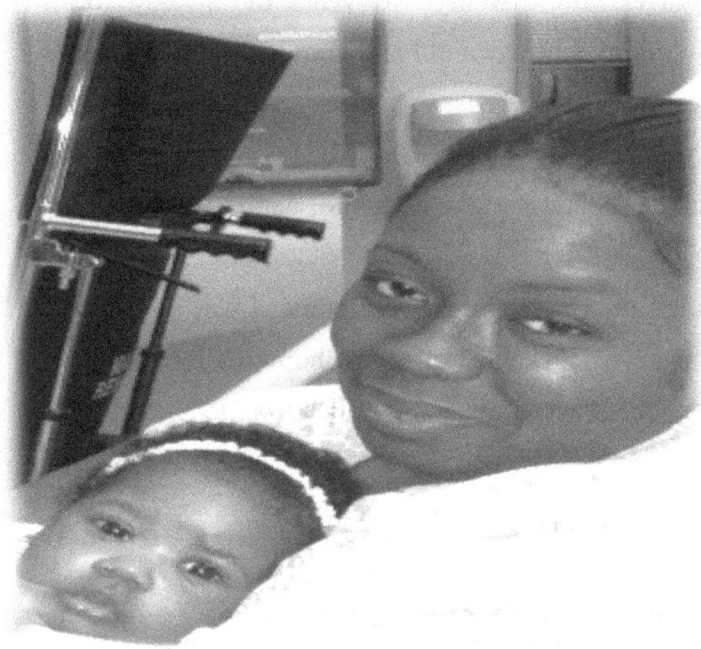

Grand-daughter visiting (great therapy)

Chapter Eight

There's No Place Like Home

Discharged from the rehab center to home was quite a transition. My family prepared and adjusted the house. A wheelchair, walker, and special equipment was needed for bathing. It was quite an experience from last time I was there two months ago.

The saying "*There's no place like home*" had become a different meaning than what it was before. A physical and occupational therapist came twice during the week. A nurse came to check on me two to three days out of the week. My mother became my caregiver preparing my meals, administering the medications, and bathing me.

She did everything for me. She also set up rotations where my sisters would come and help as well.

Once again due to the loss of oxygen to the brain and still not knowing why or what was causing it, the doctors limited my movement. They advised me not to try to move around and not to talk. They also advised me to lay still and to use a notepad and a pen to write when I needed to communicate. This was difficult to accept, it became more apparent once being in my home how helpless I really was.

Before all this occurred, I was this person that could get up and go when I was ready and do whatever I wanted to do independently for myself. I enjoyed singing and praising the Lord. I enjoyed attending church services, leading praise and worship, directing rehearsals, and attending fellowships. I also enjoyed getting water aerobics twice a week, arts, crafts, photography and hosting parties and fun activities.

As time went on, I began to feel sorry for myself and slowly fell into a level of self-pity so bad that it became depression.

I had no desire to see anyone. I was invited to go to church but was too ashamed of myself to attend. I didn't want anyone to see me the way I felt I would appear to them. Self-pity eventually became anger.

Chapter Nine

A Praying Mother

I thank God for having a praying mother. Not only a praying mother, but also a woman of faith in the Lord. No matter what the doctors said she continued to believe God was going to turn this around.

As I mentioned in chapter 6, she prayed over the medicine I was taking. She read the word and confessed the Word of God over me. I would hear her canceling the doctor's diagnosis.

My mother is also a worshipper. She worshipped the Lord, and continued to sing praises to the Lord no matter what it looked like, no matter how disconnected I seemed to be. She knew my spirit had an ear to hear.

Very often she would get in the bed and sing, *"Sonja's covered by the blood, and the devil can't do Sonja no harm"*.

She continued each day and sometimes at night. At first, I resented my situation so much I just couldn't see the hope. My natural mind was speaking so loud to me during that time.

My mother did not let my non-responsiveness affect her faith in the Lord. She said she knew God kept me even when it seemed like she was going to lose me; God gave a breakthrough and kept me. She also said she knew God was not finished with me. There was work for me to do.

You see, it was her prayer life and relationship with the Lord that kept her grounded in faith. This also gave her strength beyond her strength to remain standing in faith and not fear.

When things come unexpected and suddenly in your life or your loved one's life, you must know God. You can't wait until a crisis come to try to get to know Him. My mother knew the Lord and had the word on the inside of her.

She spoke when I couldn't speak, she worshipped in proxy for my worship and she pressed into God in faith and intercession no matter what it looked like.

I remember when my mother told me, one day as she continued to do praise and worship over me, she looked down at me lying in the bed and I began to look different. She said her heart begin to leap for joy in the Lord when she saw my bottom lip tremble in my efforts to join in with her to worship the Lord.

A Praying Mother, An Intercessor

Chapter Ten

The Prayer of Agreement

There is something about the corporate anointing. The Word of God says in *Matthew 18:19 (NKJV) "Again I say to you that if two of you agree on earth concerning anything that they ask, it will be done for them by My Father in heaven".*

There was more than two in agreement with me praying and interceding for my healing. It's so very important that you know those who labor among you. In other words, you should surround yourself with people of faith that know the Lord.

People that have a relationship with God more than with you, should be in your inner circle. My **pastor** says, "*It's all of us against the enemy!*"

When you are faced with something or in a battle, make sure the sister or brother in Christ in your life will get in the trenches with you or stand on the front line with you and fight.

It does you no good to have friends to sympathize for you. You need the people of God not moved by what they see that will be ready to go to war with you on their knees praying down the promises of God, on the wall making intercession for your breakthrough!

When the **Word of God** is spoken over a situation or a person in faith, a change will have to take place. Nothing or no one can remain the same when the **Word of God** is spoken over you.

The **Word of God** brings life!

It was such a **blessing** and a tremendous support in the spirit to have my family, my church family, Pastors Al and Didrea Moore with Westgate Church as well as many others all over the state, other states and even internationally praying in agreement for my healing. **GOD IS FAITHFUL!**

"Five of you shall chase a hundred, and a hundred of you shall put ten thousand to flight; your enemies shall fall by the sword before you".

Leviticus 26:8 (NKJV)

Chapter Eleven

Faith Comes

My mother continued to love on the Lord and to honor Him speaking the Word of God over me.

During worship time, although I didn't sing out loud, but did so under my breath, I joined her worshipping the Lord. Faith and hope began to come alive in me to God as my healer. The Word of God continued to refresh my spirit as my mother read it aloud to me. Even during times of rotation with my sisters caring for me, she gave them instructions to read the Word of God over me and to pray.

I remember from within me repenting to the Lord for being angry and asking the Lord to heal me and restore me.

I wrote out instructions for CJ, my youngest son, to get poster boards and divide them into four sections and bring to me.

Healing Scriptures from the Word of God were written on them and CJ placed them on the walls of my bedroom and throughout the house. Looking up seeing the Word of God on my wall in front of me in big letters became a strength to me and to my faith.

"Oh Lord my God, I cried out to you and you healed me." **Psalm 30:2 (NKJV)**

"But He was wounded for our transgressions, He was bruised for our iniquities; The chastisement for our peace was upon Him, And by His stripes we are healed." **Isaiah 53:5 (NKJV)**

"I shall not die, but live, and declare the works of the Lord". **Psalm118:17 (NKJV)**

"Call upon Me in the day of trouble; I will deliver you, and you shall glorify Me." **Psalm 50:15 (NKJV)**

"That it might be fulfilled which was spoken by Isaiah the prophet, saying: He Himself took our infirmities and bore our   sicknesses." **Matthew 8:17 (NKJV)**

"And He said to her, "Daughter, your faith has made you well. Go in peace, and be healed of your affliction."

Mark 5:34 (NKJV)

Just lying there in the bed not being free to just sit up and sing due to the medical issues became difficult. Hearing the Word of God spoken over me, read to me and seeing it before me on the wall was what was needed. I began to sing in a soft whisper. There was barely any volume at all. There was no loss of oxygen to my brain.

Later I began to sing in a low volume and eventually I was able to sit up and sing. There were no side effects from this. What a charge to my faith and spirit, glory to God. Later I was able to sit on the side of the bed singing and softly tapping my feet.

*"So, then **faith comes by hearing**, and **hearing by** the word of God."*

Romans 10:17 (NKJV)

Chapter Twelve

Inner Healing First

I remember thanking the Lord for allowing me to be able to worship Him, for blessing me to sit up, and not have problems with oxygen flow to my brain.

As time went on, I continued to confess the Word of God, read Scriptures on the wall, wrote journals to the Lord and read inspirational material. Not only was my family praying for me, but my church family was also praying for me and came to visit as well.

As my faith continued to grow, I got to a place where I began to ask the Lord to completely heal my body. I asked God to get me out of the wheelchair and to set me completely free. But I heard Him say to me, *"You need to be healed on the inside first."*

I didn't know really what that meant at the time because I didn't know there was something wrong on the inside.

The infirmity that I saw on the outside began with the infirmity on the inside. There's a scripture that says a broken spirit dries up the bones. Proverbs 17:22 (NKJV). There were past situations that caused pain and emotional wounds in my life that I didn't know were still there. Sometimes we can make plans for our lives and things can come along to derail those plans.

Have you ever experienced that kind of a moment in life where it's like something hit you so hard it's like the impact of a train leaving the tracks?

We move on in life even as a believer thinking it's done and we're OK. Sometimes we are ok and other times something can happen to bring that pain back up.

It's like having an injury that's healing and bandaged up, but you never remove the bandage for the healing to completely take place. And something happens, the bandage is snatched off the wound and the injury starts to hemorrhage again.

There are people hemorrhaging in the body of Christ. Some may not even be aware of the wound going on without being healed, which can cause issues physically to take place in the body.

As I began to seek the Lord concerning what was going on, I begin to pray, asking him to show me what it was about. And he began to reveal by his Spirit some things that made me weep from deep inside as I yielded my heart to him.

Somethings I had no idea I was holding onto and needed to let go and even to forgive. Sometimes we can be so busy, in doing God's business and neglect our heart.

But God is a restorer and he will heal all wounds and remove all pain that you know is there and that you may have pushed down so far that you don't remember that it's there.

I remember feeling like such a load had been lifted off me as I was being healed inside. I felt so refreshed in my spirit, more hopeful, and increasing in faith. I saw the love of God for me more clearly and I began to journal this beautiful experience.

Chapter Thirteen

My Soul Sings

-You Are Great, You Do Miracles So Great-

Since being healed on the inside, I begin to enjoy worship and reading the Scriptures even more. The depression and self-pity that were a heavy load on me was lifted. The faith scriptures from the Word of God were also placed on the walls down the hall and other rooms of the house.

I've always known God is a **healer** and His word is true. However, I couldn't grab a hold of this reality until opening myself up to Him and allowing His word to be in my hearing and to come alive in me.

Throughout this time, I was able to transition from being **bedridden** to getting in a wheelchair.

I read the scriptures along the wall down the hall and in the other rooms almost every time I passed them as a continual declaration.

My eyes were drawn to them to read them. As I continued to hear the Word of God, the word continued to make me stronger in faith. It also began to change my perception of my situation and how I saw myself. I begin to look at who's I am more than who I am.

The awareness of God's love for me also began to grow. His word will push you pass what you see, feel, and even the limitations you face. Yes, I was still having episodes of oxygen not flowing to my brain and taking 13 meds a day. *But I knew this great God was for me, and that I was not alone!*

My heart began to sing, **"You are great, you do miracles so great, there is no one else like You"**.

Worship instrumentals were played in my room and my mother and I still had worship together.

She continued to sing over me; *"Sonja's covered by the blood, Sonja's covered by the blood, Sonja's covered by the blood and the devil can't do Sonja no harm".*

I begin to sing this over myself as well.

Chapter Fourteen

No Pride – No Shame

For the Scripture says, *"Whoever believes on Him will not be put to shame."*

Romans 10:11 (NKJV)

On the way to victory sometimes requires you to push past your comfort zone. Yes, my heart was full of joy and I knew a brighter day was ahead, but leaving the house in a **wheelchair,** I did not want to do.

I remember DD, my Pastor and dear friend calling to come pick me up for a conference.

I really did not want to go because I didn't want people to see me, and I didn't want to have an episode in front of people.

Well, she came to the house to pick me up. As she waited, she said she would allow me some time to get ready. If I didn't get ready, she was coming down the hallway to my room to help me. Let me warn you, don't try this at home unless you know the person… lol.

Because of the relationship she and I have she could come at me the way she did especially because she had instruction from the Spirit of God.

After getting dressed, I came down the hallway and we left. You see in my mind, I wanted to be healed before leaving home. I wanted to walk out of my house and return to the platform singing and healed.

The conference was a blessing, an episode did happen, but they continued to pray for me through it.

Looking back, I believe that an increase in obedience was birthed in my spirit that day. We have been given a free will to choose. God will never force his love and what he has for our good upon us. We must choose to say "Yes" to him. I didn't want to leave the house, but I wanted to please God and I wanted to get all that he had for me.

The next week or so, Chris, my pastor's son, also like a son to me, started coming to the house to pick me up. I was told he did this on his own, no one asked him to come pick me up for church. This truly blessed me. Every Sunday he came to the house for me and CJ.

I sat in the wheelchair during each service toward the front. At times I was a little self-conscious and a little embarrassed because I was once the person leading praise and worship and at this point, I'm seated in the congregation in a wheelchair.

It was challenging not feeling sorry for myself as I sat watching instead of singing. My oldest son, Jeremy, lead the worship service with the team. It was a blessing to see the team. I missed them and it was very encouraging seeing them flow and carry the service as they were called to do. I felt thankful to have been a part of this growing process with them by the grace of God.

One Sunday, I heard Pastor Al say, "*Come up here Sonja*". My thought was surely he didn't say my name. CJ proceeded to get up to push me up there and I stopped him.

When Pastor said my name again, I was so embarrassed but, once again I obeyed during a moment instructed of the Lord outside of my comfort zone. This was totally outside of my comfort zone and pride had a lot to do with it as well. What will people think of me crossed my mind as I was sitting there in front of the church.

Pastor gave me the microphone, he walked away and waited. I waited for him to return to me to get it back because I was not ready.

The church seemed to be completely silent as the congregation looked at me waiting. Pastor would not return for the microphone, the church waited until my heart begin to sing and I opened my mouth and released, "*You are great, you do miracles so great, there is no one else like You*".

As the tears poured down my face and my right hand lifted to God, I began to worship Him. There was no more shame, no more pride no more anger at Pastor Al for calling me up, nor was I embarrassed. It was just me and my **great** God, as I released **worship** to Him.

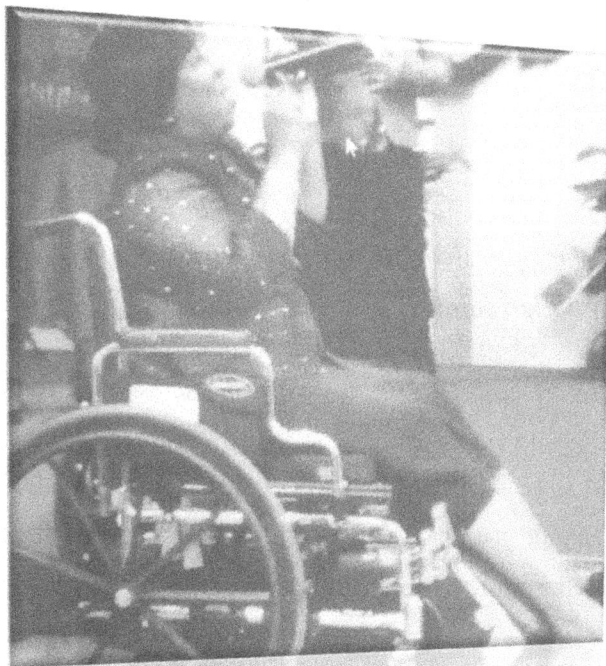

Worshipping from the wheel chair in service

Chapter Fifteen

Trusting God

"Trust in the Lord with all your heart, And, lean not on your own understanding".

Proverbs 3:5 (NKJV)

Since that time of breakthrough in my worship to the Lord, I began to lead praise and worship from the wheelchair in some of the Sunday morning services.

The songs God birthed in my heart during the time when I couldn't speak came forth as well as others. Two of the songs became like an anthem in the spirit in my life,

"I Can Worship My Way Out"

and

"I Trust You Lord"

There were times when the devil tried to distract me with my limitations, but I made up my mind to press through and keep trusting the Lord. I couldn't allow myself to focus on what I could see in the natural, nor how I would feel. At times I couldn't understand what was going on in my body but I knew God still had me. I had to know this with all my heart for myself.

Later, during devotion and worship time, a song was birthed forth entitled "Walk by Faith".

"I walk by FAITH; It's not what I see.

I'm trusting God, He'll do it for me

Through Jesus Christ, My covenant right

I enter in, it's not by sight".

Chapter Sixteen

Now Faith 1,2,3

"Now faith is the substance of things hoped for, the evidence of things not seen".

Hebrews 11:1 (NKJV)

One Sunday, in the middle of June 2012, while getting dressed for church there was a determination in my spirit of expectation from the Lord. To explain this in words is challenging, but I made up in my mind and heart that morning I was not going to church in the wheelchair and I was not going to take the walker either. It seemed insane in my natural mind, but the Word of God was strong on the inside of me and I declared until the day I walk on my own, that Sunday was the last Sunday I would take the walker and wheelchair.

Two loving friends and church members (Brian and Cheryl) arrived to pick me and my son up for service. I was asked, "Where is your wheelchair, where is your walker?" I replied, "I'm not bringing either of them with me. I just want to go to church." Then someone asked, "How will you walk?" I replied, "Can you all carry me?" They agreed.

I'm reminded of the story in the Bible in Luke 5 that talks about the men who lowered the paralyzed man down the roof and Jesus healed the man after seeing such faith. It made no sense in the natural to come to church without the wheelchair or the walker, but those with me agreed with me Hallelujah! They could have said no, we need to get your wheelchair, and your walker. They could have even decided they were uncomfortable with my decision, but they agreed.

When we arrived at the church, the ushers came out to assist and were surprised the wheelchair was not in the SUV.

They looked for the walker as well and didn't see it either. Even during this time, I know it probably seemed strange to others looking on. When you know in your heart God is speaking or instructing you, you can't look for everyone to understand or get it. They may never see what God is doing, you may not even see what God is doing, but you know you heard from him.

The power of God was so strong in the service that day. I heard Sister DD say, "Sit down everybody; sit down" she began to talk about having faith in God, and that it should be just as real as just standing up expecting God to do what he said He would do; you should expect to stand up and know in your spirit something has changed something is different. She also said no one walked in church and inspected a chair before sitting down, you had faith to just sit knowing the chair will hold you, how much more should you have faith in God.

She said, "At the count of 3, expect a change, expect things to be different in your life whatever it is."

I was on the edge of my seat. As she said, "1!" I felt such an unction from the Holy Spirit in my belly to jump up… as though someone was pulling me to my feet.

I was trying to wait until she got to three but when she said. "2!" I was standing to my feet running and it felt as though I was running on air. It felt like a strong wind hit my back pushing me forward! I felt light as a feather with such energy and strength.

Glory to God forevermore. Miraculously I was healed completely at that moment to *"The Other Side of Worship!"* God is the healer!!

Chapter Seventeen

Follow-up with the Doctor

When returning to the doctors, they did test on me, but they could not find anything wrong. One of the doctors said, "It must be a doing of the man upstairs."

Gradually one by one they began to take me off the thirteen prescriptions I was taking daily. Since that time, a few months later I returned back to work in the classroom with pre-k students. The following summer, I went on my first mission trip to Africa where I assisted the church's Missions team. It was a blessing to do praise and worship training in Africa. It was also a blessing to return and serve with an anointed group of worship leaders in the local church I attend, Westgate Church in Port Allen, Louisiana. We had our first worship conference shortly after the mission **trip** to Africa.

December of that year, God opened doors for me to record the song "Worship My Way Out".

My testimony is not for me, it's for others to be encouraged and to know God is real and He is the healer. My prayer is for others to be inspired to worship God and allow Him to minister to them in every area of their life as he has mine. To God be the glory!

"My son, give attention to my words; Incline your ear to may sayings. Do not let them depart from your eyes; Keep them in the midst of your heart; For they are life to those who find them, And health to all their flesh."

Proverbs 4:20-22 (NKJV)

After my healing, I noticed I had so many prescription bottles collected from all the medicine I was taking. For some reason, I decided prior to save them and take them back to the pharmacy to recycle.

However, when I proceeded to collect them, I heard in a still small voice, *"Why take them back for more sickness, instead find a better use for them"* so I waited not really knowing at that time what I could do with them.

At some point, days later, I remembered my Pastor sharing about his mother, Mrs. Ollie Moore being a school teacher. She would take a medicine bottle to school with nuggets from the **Bible** on slips of paper to pass out to staff to encourage them. Then the idea was birthed to fill all those prescription bottles with scriptures from the **Word of God**.

Using some of the main scriptures on healing placed on the walls in my **home,** I printed them on slips of paper and placed them in the medicine bottles. I placed a label on the cover of the bottles which said, *"Word of God-Take as many times daily as needed."*Instead of it being called prescription, it was now called *"Per-scripture."*

Chapter Eighteen

"Per-Scripture"

⭐⭐ Per-Scripture

1. Written instruction and authorization in accordance with, through and by means of the authoritative writings from the word of God (Bible).

2. The word of God given utterance (*spoken out loud*) to hear as to increase the measure of faith, spoken, however much and as often as needed concerning truths of healing obtained and purchased already through Jesus Christ.

- *And by His Stripes we are healed.*

  Isaiah 53:5 (NKJV)

- *I shall not die, but live, And declare the works of the Lord.*

  Psalm 118:17 (NKJV)

- *Oh Lord my God, I cried out you and you healed me.*

  Psalm 30:2 (NKJV)

- *that it might be fulfilled which was spoken by Isaiah the prophet saying "He Himself took our infirmities And bore our sickness."*

  Matthew 8:17 (NKJV)

- *Call upon Me in the day of trouble; I will deliver you, and you shall glorify Me.*

  Psalm 50:15 (NKJV)

- *O Lord my God, I cried out to You, And you healed me.*

  Psalm 30:2 (NKJV)

Psalm 30:2, one of the Per-Scriptures, was shared at the beginning of the book with the question, what do you think about this scripture from the Bible concerning healing? Do you believe it is real to apply in your life for today or do you believe this scripture is a part of history and only applied to writers inspired by God or characters in Bible stories?

After reading my story, I hope you agree, Yes! This scripture is real and does apply in your life and mine today.

Yes! This scripture is also a part of history and applied to writers inspired by God in history but it's still for today.

I am a writer inspired by the reality of my testimony and God healing me to share my story with you. However, I'm not a character in the bible; I'm just a person who did nothing and could do nothing to earn salvation nor healing.

It is only by the grace of God and what he has already done for me that I am free. By Jesus paying the price for me on the cross and resurrecting from the dead, Jesus removed the stain of sin and he also removed the curse of sin and the sting of death. What a divine exchange to be given life and healing for my sin.

Chapter Nineteen

Getting to The Point

No matter the attack, we must keep the praise of God on our mouth.

"I will bless the Lord at all times, His praise shall continually be in my mouth."

Psalm 34:1 (NKJV)

"Bless the Lord, O my soul; And all that is within me, bless His holy name! Bless the Lord, O my soul, and forget not all His benefits."

Psalm 103:1-2 (NKJV)

Remember and keep in mind the God of the breakthroughs of the past. He constantly brings us through. He is a faithful God.

Even though the situation may seem like it's impossible, just review the past victories. If you review, you will see you have victories.

God has brought you through so much and he has shown himself to be faithful and mighty. This is enough to continue to trust Him and to keep giving Him praise and worship.

"We are hard-pressed on every side, yet not crushed; we are perplexed, but not in despair; persecuted, but not forsaken; struck down, but not destroyed—"

2 Corinthians 4:8-9 (NKJV)

We must continue to confess the *Word of God*!

Confessing the *Word of God* will put us where we need to be in the spirit. Sometimes our faith may need to grow... read the Scriptures from your heart.

"So, then faith *comes* by hearing, and hearing by the word of God."

Romans 10:17 (NKJV)

So, as we confess the word, we're putting sound or voice to the words out loud in our hearing, as we are confessing the word we are prophesying in the spirit. We are hearing it and it helps us along with our worship.

"O Lord my God, I cried out to You, And You healed me."

Psalms 30:2 (NKJV)

Know the **Word** of God is TRUTH. Refuse to accept the diagnosis! Know the word is TRUTH!

We must always see Jesus no matter what we face no matter what we see.

"I will lift mine eyes unto the hills from whence cometh my help. My help cometh from the Lord which made heaven and earth."

Psalm 121:1-2 (NKJV)

Change how you see yourself.

"while we do not look at the things which are seen, but at the things which are not seen. For the things which are seen are temporary, but the things which are not seen are eternal. "

2 Corinthians 4:18 (NKJV)

Chapter Twenty

Truths Revealed While I Worshipped God

Did you know while worshipping God, he brings your heart to repentance and restoration?

Every day that we take that time to worship the Lord, as we commune with him our heart is being restored and connected to the Father's heart. We are being renewed day by day.

"*Godly sorrow brings repentance that leads to salvation and leaves no regret, but worldly sorrow brings death*".

2 Corinthians 7:10 (KKJV)

When I worship the Lord, it brings the stillness to who I am and the focus to who He is. Negative thoughts are shut down while worshipping and we are open to receive from the Lord while in stillness.

Be still and know that I am God!

Psalm 46:10 (NKJV)

When I worship the Lord, I'm waiting on God. Did you know the word wait also means to wrap yourself around? To be intertwined. When I worship (wait) on the Lord, I am wrapping myself into him. This will push away being discouraged because during this time, God, my Father, the Son and Holy Spirit is strengthening me.

"They that wait on the Lord, will renew their strength..."

Isaiah 40:31 (NKJV)

Worshiping God reveals his instructions and directions. God speaks to me so much during my worship time with him; I've learned that...

- He will release confirmations about things I'm praying about.

- He will reveal the unknown to bring awareness and warning.
- He will give clear instructions to which way to go and what to do.

"My sheep hear My voice, and I know them, and they follow Me. And I give them eternal life, and they shall never perish; neither shall anyone snatch them out of My hand."

John 10:27-28 (NKJV)

When I worship, I am saying, yes Lord, I accept your plan for my life.

Not the plan of the diagnosis, not even my own, but I accept God's plan and what he has already done. His plan is that I have what he has and has done for me to have.

"For I know the thoughts that I think toward you, says the Lord, thoughts of peace and not of evil, to give you a future and a hope. "

Jeremiah 29:11 (NKJV)

Going through a test or challenge, does not nullify what God has called you to do. It does not cancel the assignment or purpose God has given us. God didn't choose you and then changed his mind because we may face hardship or struggles. Keep Worshipping!

"You did not choose Me, but I chose you and appointed you that you should go and bear fruit, and that your fruit should remain, that whatever you ask the Father in My name He may give you."

John 15:16 (NKJV)

As I worship, as you worship, as we go before God and honor him every day, we are being filled every day with him. Acts 1:8 says we are receiving power; we need the strength from God He fills us and then He fills us, and

---

73

He continues to fill us again and again every day when we worship Him.

This becomes OVERFLOW! The overflow of faith, power and anointing. Our weapons become greater for spiritual warfare.

WE WIN!!

More Confession Scriptures

Here are a few additional scriptures that I recited and confessed during my time of prayer. Each are bible quotations taken from the New King James Version.

2 Corinthians 4:17

For our light affliction, which is but for a moment, is working for us a far more exceeding and eternal weight of glory.

2 Corinthians 4:8-9

We are hard-pressed on every side, yet not crushed; we are perplexed, but not in despair; persecuted, but not forsaken; struck down, but not destroyed.

Psalm 34:1

I will bless the Lord at all times; His praise shall continually be in my mouth.

2 Corinthians 4:18

While we do not look at the things which are seen, but at the things which are not seen. For the things which are seen are temporary, but the things which are not seen are eternal.

John 16:33

These things I have spoken to you, that in Me you may have peace. In the world you will have tribulation; but be of good cheer, I have overcome the world."

Revelation 12:11

And they overcame him by the blood of the Lamb and by the word of their testimony, and they did not love their lives to the death.

2 Corinthians 4:7

But we have this treasure in earthen vessels, that the excellence of the power may be of God and not of us.

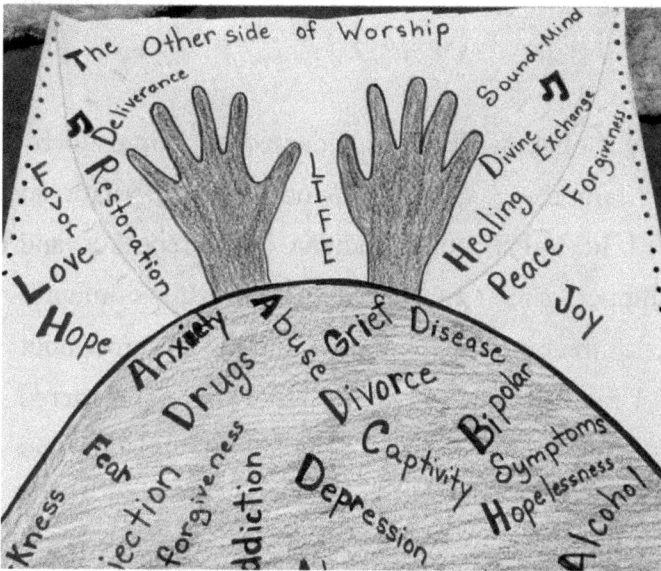

(My drawing effort of the vision of worshipping God will lift anyone from darkness to His promises in the light)

Biography

Sonja A. Bell is a Prophetic Song Writer; Worshipper, Speaker, Recording Artist and Author. She is the music minister of Westgate Church, Pastor Alfred and Didrea Moore, located in Port Allen, Louisiana. Sonja is the middle child of three daugthers born to Leon Anderson and Mary Bell.

In 2002 Sonja A. Bell was ordained as a minister by Pastor Timothy L. Crouse of Word Alive International located in Indianapolis, Indiana. As a speaker and worshipper, she's ministered in prisons; community centers, street ministry, missions and places throughout the United States. She has also ministered internationally in Liberia; Thailand; England, and France.

Sonja A. Bell is the mother of three sons, Jeremy (daughter-in-law Nacotia), Ivory and CJ. She is the elated grandmother of eight beautiful grandchildren (DeMarcus, Caleb, Karah, Jaden, Ayden, Adyana, Iviana, and Lebron.)

Products and Contact Information

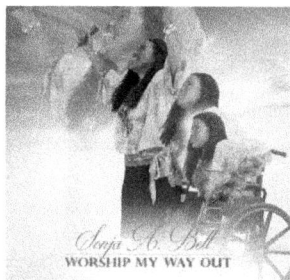

"Worship My Way Out" is a musical testament, inspired by her testimony of how God miraculously healed her from a stroke in 2012.

It is a testament of her struggles physically, emotionally, and spiritually, and is a cry for anyone that is hungry to know what to do when you have nowhere else to turn.

Released On: June 22,2016 ® 2016 Sonja A. Bell Available: Apple Music

"So Amazing" consist of songs birth during devotion and worship, as well as a combination of spontaneous and prophetic worship released seven years after her healing.

Released On: August 16, 2019 ® 2019 Sonja A. Bell Available: Apple Music, Amazon and all major platforms.

To book a ministry engagement or to order products, please email Sonja A. Bell at sonjabellmusic@gmail.com.

Notes: _____

_____

_____

_____

_____

_____

_____

_____

_____

_____

_____

_____

Notes: _____

_____

_____

_____

_____

_____

_____

_____

_____

_____

_____

Notes: _____

_____

_____

_____

_____

_____

_____

_____

_____

_____

_____

_____

Notes: _____

_____

_____

_____

_____

_____

_____

_____

_____

_____

_____

_____

Notes: _____

_____

_____

_____

_____

_____

_____

_____

_____

_____

_____

Notes: _____

_____

_____

_____

_____

_____

_____

_____

_____

_____

_____

_____

Notes: _____

_____

_____

_____

_____

_____

_____

_____

_____

_____

_____

_____

Notes: _____

_____

_____

_____

_____

_____

_____

_____

_____

_____

_____

_____

Notes: _____

_____

_____

_____

_____

_____

_____

_____

_____

_____

_____

_____

Notes: _____

_____

_____

_____

_____

_____

_____

_____

_____

_____

_____

_____

Notes: _____

_____

_____

_____

_____

_____

_____

_____

_____

_____

_____

_____

Notes: _____

_____

_____

_____

_____

_____

_____

_____

_____

_____

_____

Notes: _____

_____

_____

_____

_____

_____

_____

_____

_____

_____

_____

_____